Big Cats

Jonathan Sheikh-Miller and Stephanie Turnbull

Designed by Neil Francis

with Jayne Wilson, Glen Bird
and Stephanie Jones

Illustrated by John Woodcock

Consultants: Pat Mansard, Ridgeway Trust
for Endangered Cats and LiFeline,
Dr Nobuyuki Yamaguchi and Dr Andrew Kitchener

Series editor: Gillian Doherty

Cover picture: tiger
Title page: leopard
This page: young cheetah

Contents

4   What is a big cat?
6   Cat bodies
8   On the move
10 Senses
12 Coats and camouflage
14 Hunting
16 Killer bites
18 Cat talk
20 Getting together
22 Growing up
24 Cat habits
26 Tigers

28 Lions
30 Leopards
32 Asian leopards
34 Cheetahs
36 American big cats
38 Small wild cats
40 Under threat
42 Caring for cats
44 Myths and legends
46 Using the Internet
47 Index
48 Acknowledgements

A puma

Internet links

Look for the Internet links boxes throughout this book. They contain descriptions of Web sites where you can find out more about big cats. For links to these Web sites, go to **www.usborne-quicklinks.com** and type in the keywords "discovery big cats".

★ Some of the pictures in the book have a star symbol beside them. It means you can download the pictures from the **Usborne Quicklinks Web site**. For more information, and for safety guidelines for using the Internet, and downloading Usborne pictures, see inside the front cover and page 46.

What is a big cat?

Not everyone agrees about what a big cat is, as it's not a clearly defined scientific term. Although there are 37 kinds, or species, of cats, only a few of these are usually described as big cats.

Cat characteristics

All cats belong to a group of animals called mammals. Like most mammals, they have fur on their bodies and give birth to live young.

Cats are also carnivores, which means they eat meat or fish. They have sharp claws and teeth, which help them to catch and kill the animals they hunt for food (their prey).

Internet links

For a link to a Web site with dramatic photographs and information about cats from all over the world, go to
www.usborne-quicklinks.com

Big cat or not?

Scientists rarely use the term "big cats" without saying which cats they mean. They often include lions, tigers, jaguars, leopards, snow leopards and clouded leopards, which all belong to the "panther" group of cats. But, many people call other large cats, such as cheetahs and pumas (also called cougars, mountain lions or panthers), big cats too.

Lions are most definitely big cats. This young male is padding lazily across the grasslands of East Africa.

 Fact: Cats are descended from small meat-eating mammals called miacids that lived about 60 million years ago, at around the time the dinosaurs died out.

Cat differences

This is how a small cat usually eats.

This is how a big cat usually eats.

Big cats and small cats have a lot in common, but there are also some interesting differences between them. Some big cats can roar, while no small cats can. Most big cats also tend to feed lying down, while small cats generally feed in a crouching position.

Are big cats dangerous?

Although some big cats could easily kill people, they very rarely do. However, sometimes individual cats develop a taste for human flesh and begin hunting people regularly. Lions, leopards and tigers are the most dangerous to people.

This angry leopard would have no trouble killing a person if it decided to attack.

All over the world

Cats live in a variety of places, or habitats, including tropical rainforests, grasslands and high up on mountains. But there are no cats in the wild in either Australia or Antarctica. Wherever they are, most cats have individual areas, or territories, where they hunt and have their babies.

This puma is running across a snowy forest clearing in North America. Pumas live in both hot and cold places.

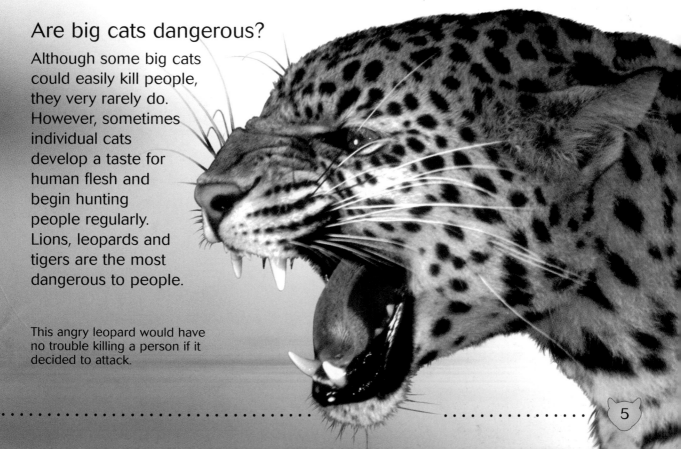

Cat bodies ....

Apart from their size and weight, there is little physical difference between a small pet cat and a large, powerful tiger. Here you can find out what they have in common.

Designed for hunting

All cats have agile, athletic bodies, which are perfect for hunting. They need to be fast enough to catch prey and strong enough to pounce on it and kill it. They use their powerful back legs to push off when they run or jump, and their front legs to grab and hold prey.

Dog-like cat

Cheetahs have slimmer bodies and longer legs than other cats. In fact, they are shaped more like a greyhound, a breed of dog, than like a cat. They are not as strong as other big cats, but they are the fastest land mammals in the world.

Here you can see how a cheetah's long, athletic body is very similar to that of a greyhound dog.

This is a leopard. The labels around it indicate some of the features that cats have in common.

A cat's upright ears can detect very quiet sounds. They can be rotated to pick up sounds from different directions.

Stiff hairs called whiskers on a cat's face help it to feel its way.

The area around a cat's nose and mouth is called a muzzle.

Claws in close-up

Cats have five claws on their front paws and four on their back paws. The fifth claw on the front paws, called the dew claw, is high up on the paw and doesn't touch the ground when cats walk. Cats use their dew claw like a thumb, to help them hold their prey. All big cats, apart from cheetahs, can pull their other claws back into pockets in their toes when walking, so that they don't wear down. On the bottom of the paws there are pads of skin which help cats to move quictly when hunting.

This picture shows where the dew claw is on a cheetah's leg.

Dew claw

★

Most cats have long tails, which they use to help them keep their balance.

Cats have loose skin under their fur. This makes it harder for rivals to cause bad bite wounds in fights.

Cats' bodies are covered in fur. Some cats have patterns such as spots or stripes on their fur.

Fact: A cat's claws are made of keratin, the same substance as your fingernails.

On the move

Big cats are fast and graceful movers. Their powerful legs help them take big strides, and their muscular bodies give them the strength to jump long distances or climb high trees.

A cheetah sprinting. When it runs as fast as it can, it takes almost three strides every second.

Built for speed

Cheetahs are excellent sprinters, able to reach 115kph (70mph). They have a flexible backbone that stretches to cover as much ground as possible, and then bends to provide the spring for the next stride.

Cheetahs also have very long tails that act as stabilizers. They help cheetahs to keep their balance while changing direction at high speeds. Cheetahs often need to do this when chasing prey.

Firm footing

Cheetahs use their extended claws to help them grip the ground. The claws act like the spikes on running shoes. Some cheetahs' paw pads are deeply ridged and this can help improve their grip, because they don't slip when they make sudden turns while racing along.

Internet links

For a link to a Web site that shows cats running and jumping, go to **www.usborne-quicklinks.com**

A cheetah starts to run by pushing up with its back legs.

It stretches right out with each bound, lifting all four legs off the ground.

★

It then draws its legs in, ready to spring again.

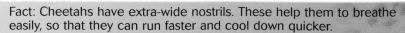

Fact: Cheetahs have extra-wide nostrils. These help them to breathe easily, so that they can run faster and cool down quicker.

Climbing high

Leopards have large, muscular bodies that are ideal for climbing trees. They hold on to the trunk with their short, strong front legs, and push themselves up the tree using their powerful back legs. As they climb they dig their claws into the trunk for extra grip.

See how this leopard climbs a tall tree, using its tail to keep its balance.

Long jumpers

A puma crouches down, ready to spring.

★ It pushes off with its back legs and stretches its body out.

Pumas and snow leopards have a stocky build and muscular back legs that are proportionately longer than those of other cats. They can jump long distances, which is useful for crossing from rock to rock in mountainous areas. Their jumping skills also enable them to hunt effectively, as they can spring onto unsuspecting prey.

Senses ....

All cats have well-developed senses that help them stay alert. Their sight and hearing are excellent, which makes them good hunters. Cats also have keen senses of smell and touch.

Good listeners

Cats' ears are very sensitive to vibrations, and detect sounds far beyond the range of human hearing. Their wide, funnel-shaped ear flaps channel sounds effectively into the ears.

Cat vision

Cats see so well because the size of their pupils (the dark circles in the middle of the eyes) can change dramatically to let in more or less light. In bright sunlight, a big cat's pupils close to tiny dots so that it can see without damaging its eyes. In dim light, the pupils open wide to let in as much light as possible.

Cheetahs hunt during the day. This cheetah's pupils have shrunk to small dots, so the cat isn't dazzled by the light.

Internet links
For a link to a Web site with lots of fascinating facts about cat senses, go to **www.usborne-quicklinks.com**

Night sight

Cats have a reflective layer, called a tapetum lucidum, at the back of their eyes, which improves their night vision. This layer reflects light back through the eye, so that the cat sees with twice as much light.

This is a diagram of a cat's eye from the side. The retina detects light twice – first as it enters the eye, then when it is reflected by the tapetum lucidum.

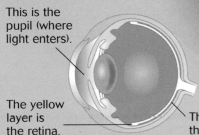

This is the pupil (where light enters).

The yellow layer is the retina.

The green layer is the tapetum lucidum.

★

The reflective layer in this leopard cub's eyes glows when a light is shone on it.

Sensitive whiskers

The long whiskers on a cat's face are very sensitive. If something touches the whiskers, or even moves nearby, cats sense it at once. Cats use their whiskers to feel their way in the dark or to investigate objects up close.

Normally a cat's whiskers stick straight out.

The whiskers can tilt down to sense objects ahead.

★

Smell detectors

Cats can smell using their noses, but they are also able to detect scents using a sensitive area, called the Jacobson's organ, in the roof of the mouth. To allow scents to reach it, a cat opens its mouth and wrinkles its nose. Scientists think that cats may need to be very close to something in order to pick up its scent like this.

A cat opens its mouth like this to detect a scent nearby.

★

Coats and camouflage......................

All cats have fur coats to keep them warm. Some have markings on their fur, and others have plain coats. Their appearance can help them to blend in with their surroundings. This is called camouflage, and it enables cats to remain hidden when hunting.

Hidden cats

Jaguars and leopards have patterns called rosettes which make them hard to see among trees, while tigers' stripes help them to hide in long grass. Lions have plain yellowish fur, which provides camouflage on the dry African grasslands.

Spot the difference

Although some species of cats have markings which make them look very similar to each other, no two cats ever have exactly the same markings.

The faces of these leopards look almost identical, but there are slight differences between them.

The markings on this tiger's head enable it to remain well hidden while choosing its moment to attack its prey.

Black cats

Most leopards and jaguars have patterned yellowish-brown fur, but some are born with black fur instead. Their fur is patterned too, but because they are black the markings are hard to see. Black leopards are often called "black panthers". Black leopards and jaguars spend most of their time in shady forests, where their dark fur gives them good camouflage.

This black leopard's camouflage is well-suited to a shady forest, but here in the open it is easy to see.

Keeping warm

Cats that live in cold places, such as snow leopards and Amur, or Siberian, tigers, have thick fur to keep them warm. Snow leopards also have long furry tails, reaching up to 90cm (3ft) in length. When resting, they curl their tails around their bodies to give them extra protection against the cold.

Furry feet

Fur is not just good for keeping out the cold. Snow leopards have thick fur between the pads on their feet. While it gives protection in snowy weather, the fur also cushions their feet as they walk over hot, jagged rocks during the summer.

Pads

This picture shows the thick fur on a snow leopard's paw.

This snow leopard's furry tail is almost as long as its body.

Hunting

Big cats are good hunters. They use a combination of cunning, patience and strength to track down and capture gazelles, antelopes, wildebeests and other prey.

A lioness creeps up on her prey, keeping her body close to the ground. She is careful not to make any sound at all.

Stealthy stalking

In places with lots of trees or long grass, big cats can sneak up on prey without being seen. This is called stalking.

When a big cat has spotted the animal it wants to catch, it inches slowly along, crouching so low that its body almost touches the ground. It gets as close to the prey as possible, then runs out of its hiding place and pounces on the animal before it can escape.

Working together

Lions sometimes hunt in groups to increase their chances of catching prey. Often they spread out and surround animals, and then run at them from different directions. This forces the animals into the paths of other lions.

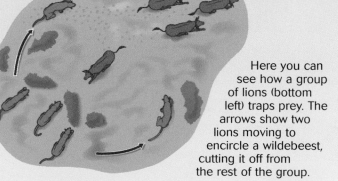

Here you can see how a group of lions (bottom left) traps prey. The arrows show two lions moving to encircle a wildebeest, cutting it off from the rest of the group.

Fact: Lions often steal prey from other cats. They wait until the prey animal has been caught and killed, then grab it for themselves.

The big chase

Cheetahs are such fast sprinters that they often chase their prey over open ground. They don't make much effort to hide as they slowly begin to approach their prey, but will sometimes freeze if the animal turns to look at them. Cheetahs only start to sprint when they get fairly close to their prey.

A mother cheetah and her cub chase a young gazelle. The mother is teaching the cub how to hunt.

Internet links

For a link to a Web site where you can watch a video clip of a cheetah chasing and killing a wildebeest, go to **www.usborne-quicklinks.com**

Lying in wait

Sometimes a big cat simply hides and waits for prey to come along, rather than tracking it down. For example, a tiger will often hide next to a waterhole. When an animal comes there to drink, the tiger springs out and catches it.

Killer bites

Big cats are swift and efficient killers. They can pounce on and kill an animal in less than a minute, and are strong enough to attack prey much bigger than themselves.

Capturing prey

A cat keeps its back paws firmly on the ground to help it drag down prey easily.

The cat forces the prey to the ground, making it fall on its side.

Big cats usually approach large animals from the back or side, to avoid being hurt by their hoofs or horns. To attack, they use their strong front legs and claws to drag an animal down.

Deadly neck bite

Big cats usually kill their prey with a single bite. The technique they use depends on the victim's size. Small animals are killed with a bite to the back of the neck. The cat slides its long teeth between the bones of the animal's neck, cutting the spinal cord leading from the brain. This kills the prey instantly.

Going for the throat

Large prey animals are too big and heavy to be held in the right position for a neck bite. Instead, the big cat bites the animal's throat and holds on tightly. Air can't get into the victim's lungs, so it is unable to breathe and soon dies.

A lioness holds down a zebra and bites into its throat, suffocating it.

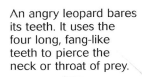

An angry leopard bares its teeth. It uses the four long, fang-like teeth to pierce the neck or throat of prey.

Terrifying teeth

Big cats normally have thirty teeth. The four long, pointed front teeth are called canines. These are used for biting and killing prey. The twelve smaller front teeth are called incisors, and are used for stripping off fur or feathers, and tearing meat from bones.

At the sides of the jaw are large, wide teeth called premolars and molars. Humans have teeth that look a bit like this. But whereas ours are rounded for chewing, cat molars and premolars have sharp edges for slicing through flesh.

Internet links

For a link to a Web site where you can learn all you need to know about tigers' teeth, go to
www.usborne-quicklinks.com

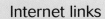

Fact: Tigers have the longest canine teeth of all big cats. The visible part can be over 5cm (2in) long.

17

Cat talk

Cats have a number of ways of communicating with each other, but not all of them involve making sounds. Slight body movements by one cat can send out clear signals to another, while smells are also a part of communication.

This male lion is roaring to tell other lions to keep their distance.

How cats roar

A roar is a deep, vibrating noise made by some big cats. Lions, leopards and jaguars can all roar, but lions are the only big cats that roar frequently. Experts aren't sure how cats roar. Most think the sound is made by air passing through the cat's voicebox, or larynx, as it breathes out forcefully. The air causes fleshy folds in the voicebox to vibrate.

When do cats roar?

Big cats often roar to warn other cats to keep away from their territories. They also tend to roar at sunrise and sunset. Sometimes cats roar when they have finished eating.

Internet links

For a link to a Web site where you can hear a lion's roar, and other animal sounds, go to **www.usborne-quicklinks.com**

Quiet tigers?

Tigers make many kinds of noises, but they can't roar like lions. Some sounds they produce are so low-pitched that humans can't hear them. Low-pitched sounds can travel long distances, so they may help tigers to communicate with each other in large, dense forests.

These jaguars are poised for a savage fight. They are growling at each other and are ready to pounce.

Body language

Cats use body language to show how they are feeling. For instance, friendly cats rub heads with each other. But angry cats thrash their tails from side to side, arch their backs to make themselves look bigger and turn the backs of their ears around to the front. They may also make loud hissing noises.

By rubbing their heads together, these male lions are showing that they like each other.

Purring

All cats can make a soft, vibrating sound called a purr, though scientists aren't sure how they do it. Small cats can purr continuously, but big cats can only purr when they breathe out. Cats tend to purr when they are happy. Purring isn't loud, and so it is a good way for mothers and cubs to communicate, without attracting interest from predators.

Scent marks

All cats use urine to mark out their territories, often spraying it against trees and rocks as they wander around. The urine has a strong scent, which is easily detected by other cats. It tells them they have entered another cat's territory.

Fact: A male lion's roar can be heard nearly 8km (5 miles) away.

Getting together

To have baby cats, known as cubs, a male and female big cat must mate with each other. Females give clear signals when they are ready to mate.

The smell test

Male cats use their sense of smell to find out if females want to mate. When females are interested, their urine contains special chemicals that tell males they are ready.

A female leopard lifts her tail up like this to spray her urine against a tree.

When a male sniffs the tree, he can tell from the smell if the female wants to mate.

Waiting for mating

Female cats decide when mating occurs. Males have to be patient and keep their distance until females let them come close to them. Males often call to females to try to persuade them to mate. When a female is ready, she shows this by rolling playfully on the ground.

This female lion isn't ready to mate and so she is angrily warning this male lion to keep his distance.

Big cat mating

To produce cubs, one of the female cat's sex cells (ova) has to join with one of the male's sex cells (sperm). When mating, the male cat crouches over the back end of the female's body in order to push the sperm inside.

Brief encounters

Mating between big cats is very quick. For instance, lions take only about twenty seconds to mate, though they may mate many times a day. Smaller cats don't mate so often, perhaps because during mating they are more vulnerable to attack.

Safe den

When female cats are almost ready to give birth, they look for a well-hidden place, or den, where they can have their cubs in safety. This might be in a cave or under bushes. It is vital that the den is well out of sight of predators.

During mating, male cats often bite the fur on the back of a female's neck like this.

Growing up ....

In their first year or two, cubs are dependent on their mother. She not only provides them with food, but also teaches them how to hunt and survive in the wild.

Helpless babies

Cubs are blind for a short time after their birth and are totally helpless. During their first few months, they feed mostly on milk produced by their mother. They suck the milk through small teats on their mother's belly.

This female leopard is showing her cubs affection by licking them, as they fight to get to her teats.

Moving dens

If a mother fears that her cubs are in danger from predators, she will move them to a new den. She does this by carrying them, one by one, between her teeth. This doesn't hurt the cubs, as she holds the loose skin at the back of the neck. Cheetahs move their dens every few days to stop predators from finding them.

A lioness carrying her cub by the skin on the back of its neck

Fact: After mother cats have moved their cubs to a new den, they sometimes make a final trip to their old den to check that they haven't left any behind.

Fighting and learning

These tiger cubs are not trying to hurt each other, but are enjoying a play fight.

Cubs spend a lot of their time play-fighting. The fights help to develop their strength and technique for when they are older and need to defend themselves against other cats, as well as catch and kill prey. If a cub doesn't have a brother or sister to fight with, its mother will sometimes play with it instead.

The first kill

Cubs instinctively know how to kill, but they need to get used to doing it, and to learn to recognize their prey. At first, their mother may bring them dead prey to eat. As they get older, cubs go hunting with their mother to learn what to do. She may catch and injure prey, but leave the cubs to kill it.

This female lion and her cubs are eating a buffalo that she has killed.

Cat habits

Cats have a lot of habits in common. For instance, they all like to keep their claws sharp for hunting, and their bodies clean. They are also very protective of their territories.

Day dreamers

Most cats sleep or rest during the day and become active at sunset. This allows them to take advantage of their excellent night vision to attack animals that can't see as well in the dark. They are also able to surprise animals that are sleeping.

Most of the lions in this group are either dozing or yawning. Lions can spend up to 20 hours a day resting.

Up to scratch

To keep their claws clean and sharp for hunting, big cats regularly scratch tree trunks. This also leaves a scent on the tree, which tells passing cats they have entered another cat's territory. Pet cats often try to sharpen their claws in the same way, by scratching furniture.

To sharpen its front claws on a tree trunk, a cheetah stretches up onto its back legs like this. ★

Spiky tongues

Cats often lick their fur to clean it. Their tongues are covered in small spikes, which make them feel rough. When a cat licks itself, the spikes act like a comb, helping to remove any loose hair. Big cats' tongues are so rough that they can lick flesh from the bones of their prey.

These tigers are fighting viciously in a river and could hurt or kill each other.

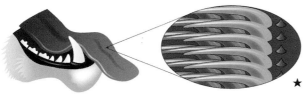

This close-up diagram shows the tiny comb-like spikes on a cat's tongue. The spikes point into the mouth.

Cat fights

A big cat's territory can be so vast that it takes three weeks to walk around it. Big cats don't like other cats moving into their territories, and will often challenge intruders aggressively. This can result in ferocious fights, which can cause serious injuries or even death.

Tigers

Tigers are huge, powerful animals that live only in Asia. Hunting and the destruction of their habitats have reduced the number of tigers in the wild, and they are now very rare.

An Amur tiger running across snow-covered ground in Russia

King of the tigers

The Amur, or Siberian, tiger, is one of the biggest cats. The males can reach up to 3m (10ft) in length, and can weigh three times as much as a person.

Amur tigers live in cold, remote areas of Russia and northern China. As protection against the biting cold, they have longer fur than other tigers. They also have a special layer of fat under the skin, which gives them extra insulation.

Big eaters

Tigers have big appetites. They can eat up to 40kg (90lb) of meat (the equivalent of a whole adult deer) in one huge meal. When looking for food, it is not unusual for tigers to walk more than 25km (15 miles) in a day.

Internet links

For a link to a Web site where you can see a video clip of tigers in the wild, study a map of where they live and send an electronic postcard of a tiger to a friend, go to **www.usborne-quicklinks.com**

Fact: Since 1900, the Caspian tiger, the Bali tiger and the Javan tiger have all died out.

Cool cats

Most tigers live in warm places, although they can find very hot weather uncomfortable. But, unlike most cats, they enjoy being in water. In India, where the summers are very hot, Bengal tigers often cool off in rivers. Tigers are good swimmers too – they are capable of crossing rivers 29km (18 miles) wide.

Man-eaters

Tigers do sometimes eat people. In the Sunderbans forest in Bangladesh and India, they kill up to a hundred people a year. To prevent attacks, people in the forest wear face masks on the backs of their heads. Tigers usually attack from behind. So if they see a face, they are unlikely to pounce because they think their prey is facing them.

By wearing a face mask on his head, this man can fool a tiger into thinking he is facing it.

White tiger

One of the rarest tigers is the white tiger from central India. These tigers are in fact Bengal tigers but, instead of having reddish-brown fur with dark stripes, they are mostly creamy white. No white tigers have been seen in the wild since 1951, although many live in zoos.

This white tiger lives in a zoo in the U.S.A. White tigers are a popular attraction for zoo visitors because of their striking appearance.

Lions

Lions are among the most fearsome animals in Africa. They live together in groups and have no predators to fear. A male lion with a mane of bushy, golden hair around its head is an impressive sight.

Pride of lions

Most big cats live alone, but lions usually live together in groups called prides. They often hunt together, so that they can each get a regular share of food. Large prides can contain more than 30 cats. Prides are biggest in places where there is plenty of food. In areas where prey is harder to find, prides can contain as few as two or three cats.

A group of lionesses hunting together. The one at the front is using her front legs to drag down a wildebeest.

Fact: In the space of nine months in 1898, two lions killed and ate more than a hundred workers who were building a railway bridge at Tsavo, in Kenya.

Busy females

Females do most of the hunting for the pride, but males are always the first to eat. The females eat once the males have finished and the cubs eat last of all. If food is short, cubs can starve to death.

Mane attraction

By the time a male lion is five years old, its mane is virtually fully grown. An impressive mane may help to attract the interest of females. It also makes a lion look big and fierce, and protects its neck during fights. As lions grow older, their manes become darker.

Asian lions

Not all lions live in Africa. In fact, until 2,000 years ago, lions lived in parts of Europe. But now these lions, called Asian lions, are found only in the Gir Forest in western India. There are only about 300 of them in the wild.

The yellow area on this map shows where Asian lions lived about 2,000 years ago. The red dot is the Gir Forest, where they live today.

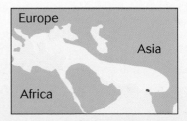

Europe

Asia

Africa

🐾
Internet links

For a link to a Web site where you can see exciting live pictures of lions in Pittsburgh Zoo, in the U.S.A., go to **www.usborne-quicklinks.com**

A male and female lion keeping a watchful eye on the open grasslands. The male (on the right) is bigger and heavier than the female, and his mane makes him look bigger still.

Leopards ....

Leopards are less than half the size of tigers, but they are very strong and can kill all kinds of prey. They are good climbers and, camouflaged by their patterned fur, can be hard to see resting in trees.

This young leopard is developing its climbing skills.

Unfussy eaters

Leopards live in many parts of Africa, as well as throughout southern Asia. No other big cat is found over such a wide area. One reason why leopards can survive in so many places is because of their varied diet. These cats will eat almost anything, from antelopes and zebras to insects and prickly porcupines.

City stalkers

Leopards are naturally shy animals. However, in parts of Africa they have become very bold, and sometimes hunt close to where people live. For example, on the edges of the city of Nairobi, in Kenya, leopards occasionally hunt very close to houses, and have even snatched pet dogs as their prey.

A leopard lazing on a large rock. Like most other big cats, leopards usually rest during the day.

Fact: Using their teeth, leopards can drag baby giraffes weighing 90kg (200lb) into trees.

A meal in a tree

When a leopard has killed its prey, it will often use its strength and climbing ability to drag the body into a tree before settling down to eat. It does this to avoid attracting the interest of other animals that might want to steal its food. If the leopard is unable to eat the kill all at once, it will keep returning to it until it is finished.

The leopard climbs a tree, holding its victim firmly by the neck.

After draping the animal over a branch, the leopard is able to eat its meal undisturbed.

Internet links

For a link to a Web site where you can see a selection of fascinating video clips of leopards in the wild, go to **www.usborne-quicklinks.com**

Rare leopard

There are only about fifty Amur, or Korean, leopards left in the wild. They live in forests near the border between Russia and China. But their habitat is being destroyed by farming and forest fires, making it hard for them to find shelter. Food is also scarce because their prey is struggling to survive too.

The patterns on this Amur leopard's fur blend in well with the dead leaves on the forest floor.

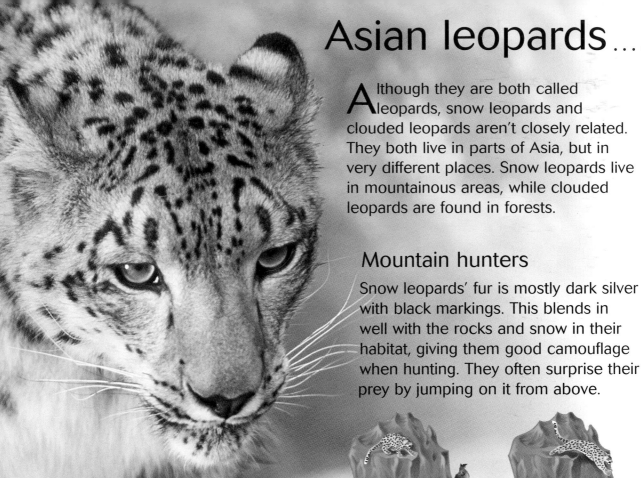

Asian leopards.......

Although they are both called leopards, snow leopards and clouded leopards aren't closely related. They both live in parts of Asia, but in very different places. Snow leopards live in mountainous areas, while clouded leopards are found in forests.

Mountain hunters

Snow leopards' fur is mostly dark silver with black markings. This blends in well with the rocks and snow in their habitat, giving them good camouflage when hunting. They often surprise their prey by jumping on it from above.

When hunting, a snow leopard crouches down on a ledge and waits for prey to appear below.

When an animal comes close, the snow leopard uses its powerful back legs to leap down onto it.

Hot and cold cats

In winter, snow leopards face very cold weather, but in summer, they experience swelteringly hot conditions. To cope with the cold, snow leopards grow longer fur and move to lower ground, while in summer they often rest in the shade.

The wide, flat shape of this snow leopard's paws spreads out its weight, so it doesn't sink when walking in deep snow.

Winter maters

Snow leopards mate during the winter, so that their cubs are born in the spring. At this time of year there is a good supply of food, and the babies grow stronger while the weather is milder. This gives them a better chance of surviving their first winter.

These healthy-looking snow leopard cubs are ten weeks old.

🐾 Internet links

For a link to a Web site where you can watch a fascinating video clip of a snow leopard in the wild, and find out more about clouded leopards, go to **www.usborne-quicklinks.com**

Clouded leopard

Clouded leopards live in the forests of Southeast Asia. They are not very big, but they have extremely long canine teeth – only slightly smaller than a lion's. Clouded leopards are good climbers and hunt monkeys and birds in trees. They are also capable of killing large prey, such as deer and wild pigs, on the ground.

Here you can see the distinctive cloud-shaped markings, from which clouded leopards get their name.

Cheetahs

Cheetahs live on open grasslands in many regions of Africa and in parts of Asia. They aren't as strong as leopards and lions, which live there too, and find it difficult to compete with them for food.

Big cat cheaters

Many people view cheetahs as big cats, but some experts think they shouldn't be included in this group because their bodies look very different from other big cats' bodies. Also, unlike most big cats, they can't roar but make high-pitched yelps instead.

Fast but weak

Although cheetahs are fast movers, they can only manage to run at very high speeds for about 300m (1,000ft). By the time they have caught their prey, cheetahs are exhausted. As a result, lions, leopards, hyenas and even vultures can easily snatch away their meal.

Here you can clearly see the cheetah's slim, athletic body shape.

Internet links

For a link to a Web site where you can find out many more facts about cheetahs, and hear what they sound like, go to **www.usborne-quicklinks.com**

Fact: In the sixteenth century, the Indian Emperor Akbar tamed cheetahs and used them to catch gazelles on hunting trips.

On the lookout

Unlike many big cats, cheetahs hunt during the day. They do this to keep out of the way of lions and leopards, which tend to hunt in the evening or at night. When hunting, cheetahs try to find areas of raised ground which will give them a good view of the open grasslands.

This cheetah has climbed onto a mound made by insects called termites to look for prey.

Cubs in danger

Cheetah cubs face a battle to survive. Within three months of their birth, most of them die. Some are snatched by predators and others starve. Female cheetahs need to make a kill almost every day to feed their cubs, but hunting is difficult and they can't always find enough food.

This female cheetah is keeping a close eye on her cub. But, when she goes off to find food, it is in danger of being taken by predators.

Hungry for gazelles

Gazelles are the most common choice of prey for cheetahs. They are smaller than cheetahs and are easily overpowered. But gazelles are fast runners and if they see a cheetah nearby, they can sometimes get away. Cheetahs usually target young or old gazelles which can't run very fast.

American big cats.....................

Although some of the best-known cats live in Africa and Asia, North, Central and South America contain many types of wild cats, including jaguars and pumas.

Jaguars

Jaguars are the third-largest of the big cats. They live in Central America and parts of South America, mostly in tropical rainforests and never far from rivers or lakes. Like leopards, they have spotted fur, but jaguars have shorter legs, larger heads and stockier bodies.

Water lovers

Jaguars hunt on the ground, in trees and even in water. They are good swimmers and often attack turtles, alligators and snakes in rivers. Jaguars also catch fish, but they can do this by fishing from the bank.

★

This is an excellent close-up view of a jaguar prowling through a forest in Belize, in Central America.

To catch fish, a jaguar finds a spot close to the water and lies in wait, keeping very still.

When a fish comes near, it swipes at it with one paw and hooks it right out of the water.

Fact: Jaguars are the only big cats that regularly kill their prey by biting through the skull.

Adaptable cats

Pumas, also called cougars, panthers or mountain lions, live all over America — from Canada all the way down to Argentina, at the southern tip of South America. Pumas live in a wide variety of habitats, including mountains, grasslands, rainforests and swamps.

Big little cat

Pumas are not usually classed as big cats, but they are often bigger than leopards and can be well over 2m (6ft) in length. They are easily capable of killing large prey such as wild deer and horses.

You can clearly see this puma's large, powerful front paws. Pumas use their front paws to grab hold of their prey.

Internet links

For a link to a Web site with amazing photographs of pumas and jaguars, and fact files about them, go to **www.usborne-quicklinks.com**

Big leapers

Pumas are very athletic and have strong back legs. They can leap the length of a bus in one bound when chasing after prey, and can jump almost 5m (16ft) straight off the ground into trees or onto rocky ledges.

A puma leaps impressively over some rocks as it chases its prey.

Small wild cats

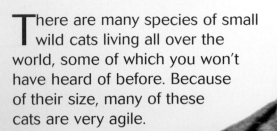

There are many species of small wild cats living all over the world, some of which you won't have heard of before. Because of their size, many of these cats are very agile.

This is a serval. It is using its very large ears to listen out for prey.

Leaping servals

Servals live in Africa. They have very good hearing, and can hear small animals rustling in the grass. From the noise, they can work out exactly where an animal is and pounce on it. Servals are also able to leap a long way off the ground, which means that they can catch birds in the air too.

A serval creeps up on birds while they are on the ground.

When the birds fly away, the serval leaps up and knocks one to the ground.

Fact: The rusty-spotted cat from Sri Lanka and India is the smallest cat in the world. It is only half the size of a pet cat.

Lynxes

Lynxes live in North America, Asia and in parts of Europe. They have short tails, distinctive tufts of fur on the tips of their ears, and long fur around their faces. Their sense of smell is thought to be particularly good – they can detect the scent of their prey 300m (1,000ft) away.

Internet links

For a link to a Web site where you can see a video clip of a margay climbing around in a tree, go to **www.usborne-quicklinks.com**

Like snow leopards, lynxes have wide paws. Here you see how they help them to walk on deep snow.

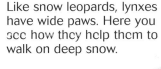

Athletic margays

Margays live in the rainforests of Central and South America. They are very athletic and are superb climbers. Their sharp claws grip branches firmly, and their flexible ankle joints enable them to move around trees almost as easily as monkeys. They can run headfirst down tree trunks, and can even run upside down along branches.

A margay crouching in a tree. These cats spend much of their time off the ground.

Under threat

Over the past hundred years, people have killed large numbers of cats and destroyed their habitats. As a result, some species of big cats have become rare and may die out (become extinct) if the current rates of destruction continue.

Panther in peril

In Florida, in the U.S.A., pumas known as Florida panthers are very rare. Towns and cities have taken over much of their habitat, and they now live a lot closer to humans than they did. They are sometimes killed by fast-moving cars as they try to cross busy roads.

No home, no hope

Every year, millions of rainforest trees are cut down for their wood, or to make way for farming. This affects cats such as jaguars and clouded leopards. As the land is cleared, their prey is either driven away or destroyed. The cats are left with little food and shelter, and so very little chance of survival.

This Florida panther lives in a zoo, safe from the many dangers that threaten these cats in the wild.

This Bengal tiger is cooling off in a river. There are now only 2,000 of these tigers left in the wild.

Tiger medicines

For thousands of years, different parts of tigers' bodies have been used in traditional Chinese medicine. For example, their tail-bones are used in creams for curing acne.

Hunting tigers is banned in most places, and few Chinese doctors still use tiger body parts. But some people do make medicines which contain them. This means that the hunters can earn a lot of money from killing tigers illegally.

These are packets of dressings containing tiger bone.

Fur trade

Clothing made from animal fur is very expensive, and hunters can make a lot of money by killing cats and selling their fur. Cats with attractive, patterned fur are especially at risk. In many places, it is now against the law to kill big cats, but illegal hunting still goes on.

Internet links

For a link to a Web site where you can find out more about many endangered animals, including tigers, go to **www.usborne-quicklinks.com**

Caring for cats

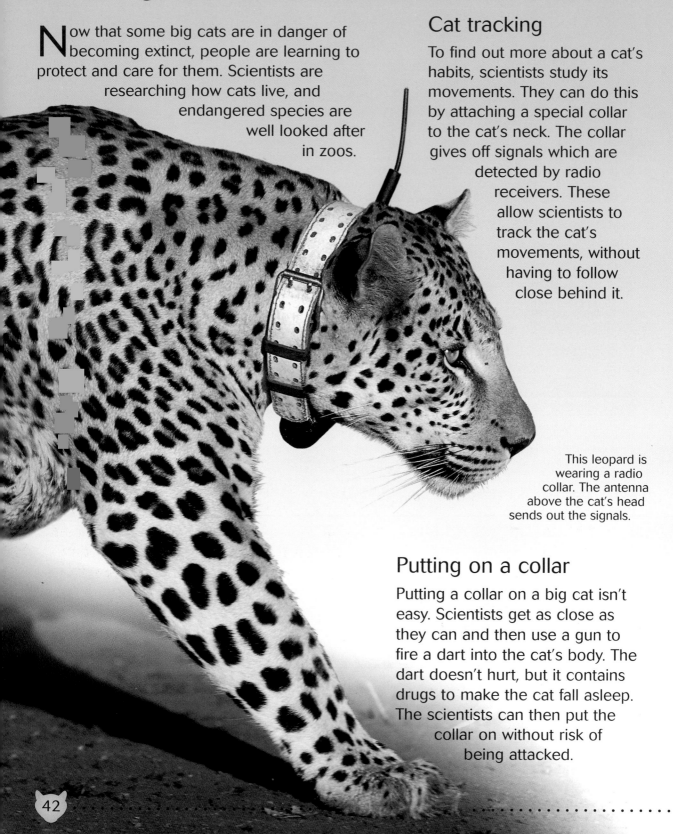

Now that some big cats are in danger of becoming extinct, people are learning to protect and care for them. Scientists are researching how cats live, and endangered species are well looked after in zoos.

Cat tracking

To find out more about a cat's habits, scientists study its movements. They can do this by attaching a special collar to the cat's neck. The collar gives off signals which are detected by radio receivers. These allow scientists to track the cat's movements, without having to follow close behind it.

This leopard is wearing a radio collar. The antenna above the cat's head sends out the signals.

Putting on a collar

Putting a collar on a big cat isn't easy. Scientists get as close as they can and then use a gun to fire a dart into the cat's body. The dart doesn't hurt, but it contains drugs to make the cat fall asleep. The scientists can then put the collar on without risk of being attacked.

Captive cats

Zoos play an important part in caring for endangered cats and giving them a safe place where they can live and breed. For example, there are now more Amur (Siberian) and South China tigers living in zoos than there are living in the wild.

Project Tiger

In 1972, Project Tiger was set up to protect Bengal tigers in India. Protected areas called nature reserves were created for them. The number of tigers almost doubled at one stage, but illegal hunting has started again and there could now be even fewer tigers than when the project started.

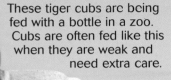
These tiger cubs are being fed with a bottle in a zoo. Cubs are often fed like this when they are weak and need extra care.

Internet links

For a link to a Web site where you can find out more about tigers and how you can help to protect them, go to **www.usborne-quicklinks.com**

On safari

Every year, thousands of people go on safaris where they travel into nature reserves to see wild animals. Countries make a lot of money from this type of tourism, and big cats are a very popular attraction. As a result, in some places, big cats are now much better protected from hunters.

These tourists are enjoying a close-up view of a male lion in Botswana, Africa.

Fact: Scientists think there are no more than 30 South China tigers living in the wild.

Myths and legends......................

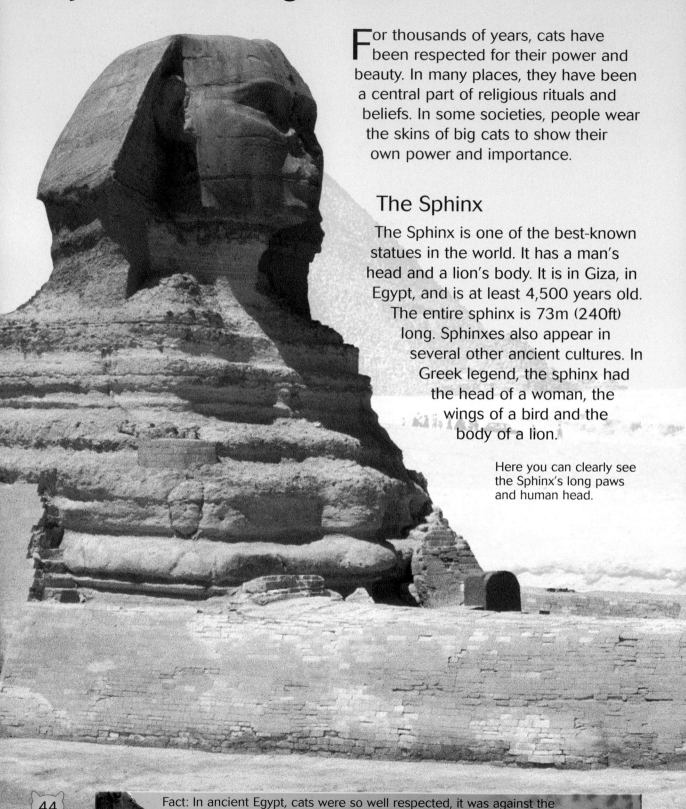

For thousands of years, cats have been respected for their power and beauty. In many places, they have been a central part of religious rituals and beliefs. In some societies, people wear the skins of big cats to show their own power and importance.

The Sphinx

The Sphinx is one of the best-known statues in the world. It has a man's head and a lion's body. It is in Giza, in Egypt, and is at least 4,500 years old. The entire sphinx is 73m (240ft) long. Sphinxes also appear in several other ancient cultures. In Greek legend, the sphinx had the head of a woman, the wings of a bird and the body of a lion.

Here you can clearly see the Sphinx's long paws and human head.

Fact: In ancient Egypt, cats were so well respected, it was against the law to kill one. A person could be put to death for doing this.

Cat gods

Some ancient Egyptian gods had cat features. For example, Bastet was a goddess of the Sun and Moon with the head of a cat, while Sekhmet, a goddess of war and punishment, had a lion's head.

A statue of the cat-headed goddess Bastet with several kittens at her feet

Dressed to impress

Because big cats are regarded as powerful hunters, people sometimes wear their skins to emphasize their own power. In South Africa, kings of the Zulu people sometimes wear leopard-skin headbands and robes.

This Zulu prince is wearing a traditional leopard-skin robe.

Jaguar gods

The jaguar has been worshipped by different peoples of Central and South America. The Olmecs, who lived in Mexico over 2,500 years ago, believed that they were descended from jaguars, and their rain god was part man, part jaguar. Today, people in this area still occasionally wear jaguar masks during festivals.

A stone figure of an Olmec jaguar spirit

Using the Internet ....

Most of the Web sites listed in this book can be accessed with a standard home computer and a Web browser (the software that enables you to display information from the Internet). We recommend:

- A PC with Microsoft® Windows® 98 or later version, or a Macintosh computer with System 9.0 or later, and 64Mb RAM
- A browser such as Microsoft® Internet Explorer 5, or Netscape® Navigator 4.7, or later versions
- Connection to the Internet via a modem (preferably 56Kbps) or a faster digital or cable line
- An account with an Internet Service Provider (ISP)
- A sound card to hear sound files

Extras

Some Web sites need additional programs, called plug-ins, to play sounds, or to show videos, animations or 3-D images. If you go to a site and you do not have the necessary plug-in, a message saying so will come up on the screen. There is usually a button on the site that you can click on to download the plug-in. Alternatively, go to **www.usborne-quicklinks.com** and click on **Net Help**. There you can find links to download plug-ins. Here is a list of plug-ins you might need:

RealPlayer® – lets you play videos and hear sound files.
QuickTime – enables you to view video clips.
Shockwave® – lets you play animations and interactive programs.
Flash™ – lets you play animations.

Help

For general help and advice on using the Internet, go to **Usborne Quicklinks** at **www.usborne-quicklinks.com** and click on **Net Help**. To find out more about how to use your Web browser, click on **Help** at the top of the browser, and then choose **Contents and Index**. You'll find a huge searchable dictionary containing tips on how to find your way around the Internet easily.

Internet safety

Remember to follow the Internet safety guidelines at the front of this book. For more safety information, go to **Usborne Quicklinks** and click on **Net Help**.

Computer viruses

A computer virus is a program that can seriously damage your computer. A virus can get into your computer when you download programs from the Internet, or in an attachment (an extra file) that arrives with an e-mail. We strongly recommend that you buy anti-virus software to protect your computer and that you update the software regularly.

> ### Internet links
> For a link to a Web site where you can find out more about computer viruses, go to **www.usborne-quicklinks.com**

Index

Words with several pages have a number in **bold** to show where to find the main explanation. Page numbers in *italic* show where to find pictures.

backbone 8
black panthers *13*, *17*
camouflage **12–13**, 30, 32
carnivores 4
cheetahs 4, *6*, 7, *8*, *10*, 15, 22, *24*, **34–35**
Chinese medicine 41
claws 4, **7**, 8, 9, 16, 24, 39
    dew claw *7*
climbing *9*, 31, 33, 39
clouded leopards 4, 32, ***33***, 40
communication 18–19
    body language 19
    growling 19
    hissing 19
    purring 19
    roaring 5, ***18***, 34
    scent 19, 24
cougars *see* pumas
cubs *11*, 20, 21, **22–23**, 29, *33*, *35*, *43*
dens **21**, 22
ears 6, **10**, 19, *38*, 39
eyes *10*, ***11***
fur 4, 7, **12–13**, 21, 25, 26, 30, 31, 32, 36, 39
    fur trade 41
gazelles 14, *15*, 34, **35**
gods (cat) 45

greyhounds *6*
habitats **5**, 26, 31, 32, 37, 40
habits 24–25
hunting **14–15**, 23, 30, 32, 33, 35, 36
    stalking 14
Jacobson's organ 11
jaguars 4, *12*, *13*, 18, *19*, ***36***, 40, 45
jaws 17
jumping **8–9**, 32, 37
leopards 4, 5, **6–7**, 9, *11*, *12*, *13*, *17*, 18, *20*, 22, ***30–31***, 34, 35, 36, 37, 42
    Amur/Korean *31*
    skins 45
lions 4, 5, 12, *14–15*, *16*, *18*, *19*, *20*, *21*, *22*, 23, *24–25*, **28–29**, 33, 34, 35, 45
    Asian 29
    prides 28
lynxes *39*
mammals **4**, 6
mane 28, ***29***
margays *39*
mating **20–21**, 33
miacids 4
mountain lions *see* pumas
muzzle *6*
nose *6*, 11
nostrils 8
Olmecs 45
panther group 4
panthers *see* pumas
paws **7**, 8, *13*, *32*, *37*, 39
    pads **7**, 8, *13*

play-fighting 23
Project Tiger 43
pumas 4, *5*, *9*, 36, ***37***, *40*
    Florida panther *40*
radio collar *42*
running **8**, 34
rusty-spotted cats 38
safaris *43*
senses 10–11
    hearing **10**, 38
    sight 10, 11
    smell 10, **11**, 20, 39
    touch 10, **11**
servals *38*
snow leopards 4, 9, *13*, ***32–33***, 39
Sphinx *44*
swimming 27, 36, *41*
tail 7, 8, 9, *13*, *19*, 39
tapetum lucidum *11*
teeth 4, **16–17**, 22, 30, 33
territories 5, 18, 19, **25**
tigers 4, 5, 6, *12*, 13, 15, 17, 18, *23*, 25, **26–27**, 30, *41*, *43*
    Amur/Siberian *13*, *26*, 43
    Bali 26
    Bengal *27*, *41*, 43
    Caspian 26
    Javan 26
    South China 43
    white *27*
tongues *25*
tracking 42
whiskers *6*, ***11***
zoos 43
Zulu people *45*

Acknowledgements . . . .

Every effort has been made to trace the copyright holders of the material in this book. If any rights have been omitted, the publishers offer to rectify this in any subsequent editions following notification. The publishers are grateful to the following organizations and individuals for their permission to reproduce material (t=top, m=middle, b=bottom, l=left, r=right):

Cover © Digital Vision; **P1** © Digital Vision; **P2** © Bruce Coleman Inc.; **P3** © Darrell Gulin/CORBIS; **P4** © Digital Vision; **P5** (mr) © Joe McDonald/CORBIS, (br) © David A. Northcott/CORBIS; **P6-7** © Alain Compost/Bruce Coleman; **P8** © Gallo Images/CORBIS; **P9** © Digital Vision; **P10** © Digital Vision; **P11** © Digital Vision; **P12** (tm) © Anup Shah/Nature Picture Library, (tr) © Torsten Brehm/Nature Picture Library, (b) © W. Perry Conway/CORBIS; **P13** (t) © Lee Green/CORBIS, (b) © Tom Brakefield/CORBIS; **P14-15** © Peter Blackwell/Nature Picture Library; **P15** © Tom Brakefield/CORBIS; **P16** © Norman Tomalin/Bruce Coleman; **P17** © Bruce Coleman Inc.; **P18** © Lynda Richardson/CORBIS; **P19** (t) Luiz Marigo/Still Pictures, (b) © Alissa Crandall/CORBIS; **P20** © Joe McDonald/CORBIS; **P21** © Mary Ann McDonald/CORBIS; **P22** (l) © Richard Du Toit/Nature Picture Library, (r) © Tom Brakefield/CORBIS; **P23** (t) George D. Lepp/Science Photo Library, (b) © Peter Johnson/CORBIS; **P24-25** © Peter Blackwell/Nature Picture Library; **P25** © Gallo Images/CORBIS; **P26** © Tom Brakefield/CORBIS; **P27** (t) © Associated Press/John Moore, (b) © Kevin Fleming/CORBIS; **P28** © Yann Arthus-Bertrand/CORBIS; **P28-29** © Pictor International/Pictor International, Ltd./PictureQuest; **P30** (t) © Digital Vision, (b) © Digital Vision; **P31** © Tom Brakefield/CORBIS; **P32** © Stuart Westmorland/CORBIS; **P33** (m) © Terry Whittaker/CORBIS, (b) © Alain Compost/Bruce Coleman; **P34** © Simon King/Nature Picture Library; **P35** (l) © Gallo Images/CORBIS, (r) © Pete Oxford/Nature Picture Library; **P36** © Lynn M. Stone/Nature Picture Library; **P37** (t) © D. Robert & Lorri Franz/CORBIS, (b) © John Conrad/CORBIS; **P38** © Torsten Brehm/Nature Picture Library; **P39** (t) © D. Robert Franz/CORBIS, (b) © Kevin Schafer/CORBIS; **P40** © Lynn M. Stone/Nature Picture Library; **P41** (t) © Yogi, Inc./CORBIS, (b) Andy Rouse/NHPA; **P42** © Gallo Images/CORBIS; **P43** (t) © Reuters/John Sommers, (b) Daryl Balfour/NHPA; **P44** © Wolfgang Kaehler/CORBIS; **P45** (t) © The British Museum, (ml) © AKG London/Erich Lessing, (r) © Gallo Images/CORBIS

Photographic manipulation by John Russell.

. . . .